Hello Friends !
Thank you for your support by purchasing my book.

I am Marta, (Maremi Small Art).
My biggest passion is being creative and sharing my love for art with others.
I take great pride in encouraging and inspiring others through my art video tutorials
on my YouTube channel (Maremi SmallArt).
I am grateful for having an opportunity to be able to walk
next to beginners in their creative journey.
There is no better reward than seeing others spread their wings.

I always wanted to create a book that will have the most beautiful elements
for my art journaling projects. Over the years I have been collecting ideas, inspirations
and making art that reflects my unique perspective
and creative visions. I really hope you will enjoy every single page
in this book and that it will inspire you in your own creative journey!

Yours, Marta

Be sure to check my other books:

SCAN this QR code with your phone
point the camera at the QR code & hold steady
A popup link will appear, tap it to open the content
& discover all my other books in one place

TRUST THE JOURNEY | CHOOSE WITH COURAGE | LOVE

LOVE CONQUERS ALL | EMBRACE THE UNKNOWN | SMILE

SEEK THE LIGHT | CREATE YOUR PATH | THANK YOU

ENJOY THE MOMENT | DREAM WITHOUT LIMITS

HAPPY BIRTHDAY | I LOVE YOU | WITH SYMPATHY

HAPPY ANNIVERSARY | BEST WISHES | WITH LOVE

HAPPY BIRTHDAY | MY DEEPEST CONDOLENCES | LOVE

CONGRATULATIONS | WELL DONE | BEST WISHES

BONUS DELIGHT

MINI FAIRY COLLECTION

BONUS PAGE

Are you curious to see
what's inside the already published books ?
Those elements are a perfect example what to expect!

I hope you will enjoy a unique
set of elements created for this book only.

Wishing you a delightful time as you make art, Marta x

I would love to invite you to visit my YouTube channel.
Scan this QR code using your phone and watch many inspirational videos:

Free Video Tutorials

Maremi SmallArt

Collage in tiles - industrial edition

join our Facebook group:

Cut & Collage - 📖 Art Journaling with Maremi #maremicollagebooks

Maremi SmallArt

Maremi's Small Art

maremis_small_art

maremi_simple_craft

online store: maremismallart.com

Printed in France by Amazon
Brétigny-sur-Orge, FR

32973343R10040